California Bucket List
Adventure Guide & Journal

*Explore 50 Natural Wonders You Must
See & Log Your Experience!*

Bridge Press

Bridge Press
dp@purplelink.org

Please consider writing a review!
Just visit: purplelink.org/review

ISBN: 978-1-955149-15-0

FREE BONUS

Find Out 31 Incredible Places You Can Visit
Next! Just Go To:

purplelink.org/travel

Contents

How to Use This Book

Welcome to your very own adventure guide to exploring the natural wonders of the state of California. Not only does this book layout the most wonderful places to visit and sights to see in this vast state, but it also serves as a journal so you can record your experience.

Adventure Guide

Sorted by region, this guide offers 50 amazing wonders of nature found in California for you to go see and explore. These can be visited in any order, and this book will help you keep track of where you've been and where to look forward to going next.

Each section describes the area or place, what to look for, how to get there, and what you may need to bring along. A map is also included so you can map out your destinations.

Journal Your Experience

Following each location description is a blank journal page. During or after your visit, you can jot down significant sights encountered, events confronted, people involved, and memories of your adventure. This will add even more value to your experience and keep record of your time spent witnessing the greatest wonders of California.

GPS Coordinates

As you can imagine, not all of the locations in this book have a physical address. Fortunately, some of our listed wonders are either located within a National Park or Reserve or are near a city, town, or place of business. For those that are not associated with a specific location, it is easiest to map it using GPS coordinates.

Each adventure in this guide will include both the GPS coordinates along with general directions on how to find the location.

Preparation
It is important that you are prepared for poor cell signals. It is recommended to route your location and ensure that the directions are accessible offline. Luckily, Google Maps can be downloaded for offline access without an internet connection. Depending on your device and the distance of some locations, you may need to travel with a backup battery source.

If possible, stop at a visitor's center to check on trail conditions and to grab a map. Rain, snow, high tides, wildfires, rockslides, and other forces of nature can cause trails to become impassable.

Also, keep in mind that some areas will not include running water, restroom facilities, electricity, or gas stations. Always prepare for your trek, and remember to leave no trace. Now let's get to exploring!

About California

The gorgeous state of California has been drawing people from near and far for hundreds of years. The Golden State earned its official nickname from the Gold Rush in 1848 that brought 300,000 people to the territory. On September 9, 1850, California became the 31st state of the United States of America and soon became the most populated U.S. state.

Third Largest State

Stretching for nearly 900 miles, California is the third-largest state by land area in the U.S. It reaches from the U.S. state of Oregon to Mexico and boasts a total land area of 163,694 miles. The United Kingdom could fit inside the state of California one-and-half times. Although highly populous, most of California's residents live near one of its four largest cities: Los Angeles, San Diego, San Jose, and San Francisco.

Landscape and Climate

Covering that much area offers a stunning variety of terrains, climates, and phenomena found in nature, including cliff-lined beaches, mountains, valleys, deserts, farmland, and forests. In fact, the highest and lowest points of the contingent 48 states are both located in California.

California is home to some of the most exceptional trees in the world, several mountain ranges, millions of acres of farmland, and an abundance of natural beauty. The diversity of landscapes and nature includes a diversity of wildlife, too. Great expanses of wilderness and several national parks provide habitats for thousands of species of animals and plants to experience.

The climate varies by the area, depending on how far north versus south and your proximity to the ocean. A majority of California's climate is considered the Mediterranean, meaning warm, dry summers and mild, wet winters. Cities on the coast experience maritime climate, while inland locations like Central Valley can be quite hot in the summer. Very cold climates are found in the higher mountainous areas, but there are also desert regions such as Death Valley.

Map of California

Northern Region

Bumpass Hell

Appropriately named, Bumpass Hell is 16 acres of boiling springs, mud pots, fumaroles, and steam vents. Bumpass Hell is the most popular geothermal area in Lassen Volcanic National Park.

Bumpass Hell contains Big Boiler, the biggest fumarole in the park and one of the hottest in the world. The colorful soils and fool's gold are neat to see, and the 2.6 mile round trip trail is scenic. Prepare for the smell of sulfur once you arrive at the otherworldly landscape of Bumpass Hell.

Best time to visit: Summer or fall, June-October

Pass/Permit/Fees: $30 per vehicle or $25 per motorcycle to enter Lassen Volcanic National Park, $15 if, on foot, horse, or bike, and during the winter, entrance fees are $10.

Closest city or town: Mineral, California

How to get there: The parking area is located near the southern entrance of Lassen National Park. The trailhead starts there and winds up the rocky slopes of Bumpass Mountain, reaches an overlook, and then descends into Bumpass Hell.

GPS Coordinates: 40.4582° N, 121.5011° W

Did you know? The striking colors occur due to minerals in the waters of the area, with orange and yellow soils against bright blue and emerald green waters.

Journal:

Date(s) Visited:

Weather
conditions:

Who you were with:

Nature observations:

Special memories:

Burney Falls

Within the Cascade Range and Modoc Plateau, natural region is McArthur-Burney Falls Memorial Park, home to the 129-foot Burney Falls. While not the largest or highest waterfall in California, it is magnificent. The water flows year-round because the waterfall is fed by both the creek above and an underground river behind the falls, which provides lovely cascading water scenery.

There are five miles of trails within the park to explore, including the Burney Falls Trail Loop, which is suitable for all skill levels of hikers. It starts at the bottom of the falls, passes over the Rainbow Bridge, then above the falls, and loops back to the foot of the falls.

Best time to visit: Spring to fall

Pass/Permit/Fees: $10 per vehicle day-use, $30 overnight with one vehicle, and +$10 for additional overnight vehicles.

Closest city or town: Redding, California

How to get there: From Redding, take I-5 North toward Weed/Portland. Take exit 680 for CA-299/Lake Blvd. Keep right at the fork and merge onto CA-299 East. Turn left onto CA-89 North, drive six miles, and the park will be on your left.

GPS Coordinates: 41.0121° N, 121.6518° W

Did you know? Theodore Roosevelt referred to Burney Falls as the "eighth wonder of the world."

Journal:

Date(s) Visited:

Weather conditions:

Who you were with:

Nature observations:

Special memories:

Emerald Bay Beach

A national natural landmark, Emerald Bay Beach is Lake Tahoe's crown jewel. The depth and incredible clarity of the water offer a surreal landscape of deep turquoise blues and greens set against the mountainous backdrop.

Inspiration Point is an iconic stop along Highway 89 that overlooks the vibrant landscape of the area. It also offers a view of Fannette Island right in the middle of the bay.

Trail hiking, water sports, and kayaking offer visitors the chance to explore the region from high and low. Emerald Bay is one of the most photographed spots in the U.S.

Best time to visit: Springtime

Pass/Permit/Fees: $10 entrance fee into Emerald State Park

Closest city or town: South Lake Tahoe, California

How to get there: Accessed via boat or Vickingsholm hiking trail. To get to the trailhead, take Hwy. 89 North from South Lake Tahoe, about nine miles to the parking lot to the right.

GPS Coordinates: 38.9542° N, 120.1104° W

Did you know? Emerald Bay is also an underwater state park as of 1994. Artifacts lie underwater, including boats, launches, and barges used in the lake, and are viewable via scuba diving.

Journal:

Date(s) Visited:

Weather
conditions:

Who you were with:

Nature observations:

Special memories:

Fern Canyon

A narrow canyon lined in lush green ferns and mosses with Home Creek running through the middle, Fern Canyon is a magical place to traverse. Located in the Prairie Creek Redwoods State Park, Fern Canyon is most known for its 50-foot high towering plant walls.

An easy 1.1-mile hike takes you through coastal forests and to hidden waterfalls. It is a wet journey, so wear shoes suitable for water. Depending on the time of year, be cautious of Roosevelt Elk.

Best time to visit: Visit in June through September, when the creek isn't as high, and the greenery is still luscious.

Pass/Permit/Fees: $8 park entrance fee, cash only

Closest city or town: Orick, California

How to get there: 1) A moderate five-mile hike on the James Irvine Trail from the Prairie Creek Redwoods Visitor Center or 2) From Hwy. 101 at Orick, drive 10 miles on the unpaved access dirt access road called Davidson Rd. Beware, there many blind turns and stream crossings.

GPS Coordinates: 41.4016° N, 124.0650° W

Did you know? Steven Spielberg considered Fern Canyon an "unforgettable natural wonder" and chose it as a filming spot for *Jurassic Park 2*.

Journal:

Date(s) Visited:

Weather
conditions:

Who you were with:

Nature observations:

Special memories:

Founders Grove

Located along the Avenue of the Giants, Founders Grove is a half-mile hike full of luscious green moss and enormous redwood trees. It is one of many redwood hikes and is the most-visited grove in Humboldt Redwoods State Park.

The trees have grown incredibly giant thanks to the shielding provided by the 3,000-foot mountains to the west. The summer fog keeps the trees watered in place of irregular rainfall.

The centerpiece of the grove is the Founders Tree, which is 346 feet tall and stands taller than the trees around it. There is a walk-up platform to allow visitors to get close and marvel at the massive size of this tree. There is a tree called Hollow Tree, which is literally a standing tree that can be walked into due to the large hollow.

Best time to visit: Before 8 a.m. or winter

Pass/Permit/Fees: Free parking

Closest city or town: Eureka, California

How to get there: From Hwy. 101 and take Exit 663. Turn onto Avenue of Giants and then onto Dyersville Loop Rd. Parking is across from the trailhead.

GPS Coordinates: 40.3513° N, 123.9273° W

Did you know? The immense, fallen tree, the Dyersville Giant, is a notably huge fallen tree in the forest and fell in 1991. It is 370 feet long and believed to be 1,600 years old.

Journal:

Date(s) Visited:

Weather conditions:

Who you were with:

Nature observations:

Special memories:

Glass Beach

Although there is human involvement in this attraction, what nature did with it is what is truly amazing. At one time in the early to mid-1900s, this site was used as a trash dump, which is where the glass originates. Over time, the ocean broke and flattened the glass into smooth, colorful glass pieces. The sea glass mixed in with the pebbles on the beach to create Glass Beach.

There are actually three beaches in the area that feature colorful, smooth sea glass. Unfortunately, the glass is frequently taken from the beach by visitors, although it is illegal to do so. It is admirable how nature repurposed glass into something unique, so let's keep it around for years to come.

Best time to visit: June-October

Pass/Permit/Fees: Free

Closest city or town: Fort Bragg, California

How to get there: From Fort Bragg, drive north on CA-1 and take a left onto W. Elm St. for 0.2 miles. The parking area is on the left.

GPS Coordinates: 39.4526° N, 123.8135° W

Did you know? Glass Beach is thought to have the highest concentration of sea glass in the world.

Journal:

Date(s) Visited:

Weather
conditions:

Who you were with:

Nature observations:

Special memories:

Half Dome

Perhaps the most recognizable landmark in Yosemite National Park, Half Dome, is a granite dome formation found at the eastern end of Yosemite Valley. It rises 4,737 feet above the floor of the valley. The sheer vertical face of one side starkly contrasts the rounded dome and is viewable from several vantage points around Yosemite National Park, including Tunnel View and Glacier Point. The more adventurous opt to hike to the top of it, and it is an extremely strenuous day hike. You can only climb Half Dome when the cables are up, which are used for the last 400 feet of the climb. The entire Half Dome trail is 17 miles round trip.

Best time to visit: May-October, if climbing. Roads and trails are closed the majority of the year due to snow.

Pass/Permit/Fees: Cable route permits are awarded via lottery. Entering the lottery costs $10 and covers six permits per application. Winners pay an additional $10 per person. Visitors also pay the park's entrance fee: $30 in summer and $25 in winter.

Closest city or town: Merced, California

How to get there: Hwys. 41, 140, and 120 provide access to Yosemite Valley all year, but tire chains may be required in the winter months.

GPS Coordinates: 37.7459° N, 119.5332° W

Did you know? The first ascent of Half Dome was by George G. Anderson in 1875.

Journal:

Date(s) Visited:

Weather conditions:

Who you were with:

Nature observations:

Special memories:

Lava Beds National Monument

At over 46,000 acres, this park features more than 700 caves, with around 20 being accessible. Volcanic eruptions have created a diverse and rugged landscape. The caves are lava tubes formed from past eruptions and are the main attraction.

Most of the developed caves are located along Cave Loop. Mushpot Cave is nearby and is the only lighted cave at Lava Beds. Caves are listed by difficulty in three categories: least, moderate, and most challenging. Along with Mushpot, Crystal Cave, Sunshine Cave, Golden Dome Cave, and Skull Cave are all popular attractions.

The 13 above-ground trails feature incredible views of the lava fields, wilderness, and wildflowers when in bloom. There are also cinder cones, pit craters, and spatter cones around the area.

Best time to visit: Any time

Pass/Permit/Fees: $20 entry fee

Closest city or town: Tulelake, California

How to get there: From I-5, take U.S. 97 north and turn right California Hwy. 161, or Stateline Rd. Travel east on CA 161 to Hill Rd. Turn right on Hill Rd., following monument signs. Travel south on Hill Rd. 10 miles to Lava Beds.

GPS Coordinates: 41.7749° N, 121.5070° W

Did you know? This area also includes historical sites of the Modoc Indian War of 1872-1873.

Journal:

Date(s) Visited:

Weather
conditions:

Who you were with:

Nature observations:

Special memories:

Mono Lake

Mono Lake is an ancient saline lake famous for its tufa towers. Tufas are soft, porous rock formations, and the tufa towers form beneath Mono Lake in the calcium-rich springs that seep up into the lake bottom. The calcium comes into contact with the carbonites in the lake, and a chemical reaction occurs, resulting in limestone

The water in the lake is incredibly dense due to the high salt content. Because of the brine shrimp and alkali flies, Mono Lake draws flocks of birds. The tufa towers standing along the shoreline of the lake make for great photos. You can also kayak on the lake.

Best time to visit: December-March

Pass/Permit/Fees: $10

Closest city or town: Lee Vining, California

How to get there: At the end of Tioga Pass Rd. Best to access on the southern side. From Lee Vining, take Hwy. 395 to Hwy. 120 East. Watch for signs that lead to the parking lot at the trailhead.

GPS Coordinates: 38.0128° N, 118.9762° W

Did you know? Tufas here reach heights of 15 to 20 feet above water and over 30 feet underwater.

Journal:

Date(s) Visited:

Weather
conditions:

Who you were with:

Nature observations:

Special memories:

Mount Shasta

If mountain climbing is on your bucket list, the peak of Mount Shasta should interest you. It is the largest volcanic peak in the contiguous United States, and at an elevation of 14,000 feet high, it is the fifth highest peak in California.

Skilled mountain climbers may seek to summit the volcano's peak but beware of the skill and equipment required. There are also easier paths full of wildflowers and forests for an alternate scenic route. The scenic 14-mile drive is also highly recommended, and there are seven viewpoints around the area to simply take in the sight of the mountain from a distance. Lake Siskiyou is a classic, where the mountain towers over the lake, and on a clear day, reflects off of the water.

Best time to visit: April-September

Pass/Permit/Fees: Each person entering the wilderness needs a free Wilderness Pass. If you plan to climb above 10,000 feet, you will also need a Summit Pass, which costs $25 per person and is valid for three days.

Closest city or town: Mount Shasta, California

How to get there: By highway, take I-5 to Lake Street at Mount Shasta City. Follow Lake St. east to Everitt Memorial Hwy.

GPS Coordinates: 41.4099° N, 122.1949° W

Did you know? Mount Shasta has been the subject of an unusually large number of legends and myths.

Journal:

Date(s) Visited:

Weather
conditions:

Who you were with:

Nature observations:

Special memories:

The Painted Dunes

Lassen Volcanic National Park is home to the Painted Dunes, a landscape that looks like a colorful watercolor painting. One of nature's masterpieces, the sand has red and orange blotches, speckled with trees and offset by the black volcanic rock. The Painted Dunes are pumice fields formed when the area's volcanoes released layers of volcanic ash that oxidized after falling atop a lava flow while still hot. The summit atop Cinder Cone offers the best view of the landscape, but it is a challenging climb because of loose rocks. Round trip, the hike up Cinder Cone is 4 miles long, and climbers are rewarded with scenic views in all directions. From the summit, Prospect Peak, Lassen Peak, Snag Lake, the Fantastic Lava Beds, and the Painted Dunes are all visible.

Best time to visit: Summer and fall

Pass/Permit/Fees: $30 per vehicle, $25 per motorcycle, and $15 per individual.

Closest city or town: Old Station, California

How to get there: From the intersection of State Hwy. 44 and State Hwy. 89, continue east on 44 for 11 miles. Watch for a sign for Butte Lake Campground and turn right. Located in the northeast corner of the park, the trailhead is near Butte Lake.

GPS Coordinates: 31.9565° N, 106.4046° W

Did you know? Lassen Volcanic National Park is one of the few places in the world that contains all four types of volcanoes.

Journal:

Date(s) Visited:

Weather
conditions:

Who you were with:

Nature observations:

Special memories:

Petrified Forest

Approximately 3.4 million years ago, Mount St. Helena erupted and began the creation of the Petrified Forest in Sonoma County, California. The largest preserved trees in the world are found in the Petrified Forest. These giant redwood trees have fossilized due to lying beneath volcanic ash for millions of years.

The trails here offer the unique experience of journeying through a preserved ancient forest. It is the only petrified forest from the Pliocene Epoch.

There are trails in the forest that provide views of Mt. St. Helena, the extinct volcano whose powerful eruption knocked down the prehistoric forest of Redwoods. The Petrified Forest Walk is 0.9 miles. There are guided tours Wednesdays-Sundays and self-guided tours all day long during open hours.

Best time to visit: Spring and fall

Pass/Permit/Fees: $10

Closest city or town: Calistoga, California

How to get there: From Santa Rosa, head south on Hwy. 12, turn left onto Calistoga Rd., which becomes Petrified Forest Rd.

GPS Coordinates: 35.0037° N, 109.7889° W

Did you know? The same family, the Bockees, have operated and maintained the forest for more than 100 years.

Journal:

Date(s) Visited:

Weather
conditions:

Who you were with:

Nature observations:

Special memories:

Redwood Forest National Park

One of three parks in the Redwood National and State Park System, this area is home to the tallest trees in the world.

In a remote grove is Hyperion, the current world's largest tree, discovered in 2006. It stands at 379.1 feet tall, making it six stories higher than the Statue of Liberty.

There are ample places to camp at the developed campgrounds or the backcountry camps at this park. Since there are dozens of trails full scenic routes, you might want to stay awhile.

Best time to visit: Any time of year

Pass/Permit/Fees: $35 developed campground fee, reservations required. Free permits are required for backcountry camping (with the exception of Gold Bluffs Beach, $5 per person per night).

Closest city or town: Eureka, California

How to get there: The parklands are 50 miles long and stretch from Crescent City to Orick, California. It is generally oriented along Hwy. 101 between the two cities. Park headquarters are in Crescent City, California.

GPS Coordinates: 41.2132° N, 124.0046° W

Did you know? Redwood National and State Parks contain 45% of the remaining protected old-growth redwoods of California at 38,000 acres.

Journal:

Date(s) Visited:

Weather conditions:

Who you were with:

Nature observations:

Special memories:

Subway Cave

20,000 years ago, the ground broke apart, and volcanic rock burst out to create Hat Creek Lava Flow. Exposed to the air above ground, the top of the lava flow cooled and solidified, but molten rock continued to flow, creating a lava tube. The molten lava has long since drained away, and we can now walk through a lava tube.

Subway Cave is a section of that lava tube located between two areas where the ceiling caved in and is accessed via a metal staircase into the underground tube. The cave is located on the self-guided Subway Cave Trail, a 0.75-mile loop trail. It is cool and dark in the cave, so bring a flashlight and jacket and take note of the jagged ground.

Best time to visit: Only open in May-October

Pass/Permit/Fees: Free

Closest city or town: Old Station, California

How to get there: The trailhead is less than half a mile from the junction of Hwy. 89 and Hwy. 44 in Old Station. Take the Subway Cave access road on the east side of Hwy. 89, across the road form Cave Campground

GPS Coordinates: 40 41.126°N, 121 25.141°W

Did you know? The opening to the cave begins before the descent and is called "Devil's Kitchen."

Journal:

Date(s) Visited:

Weather conditions:

Who you were with:

Nature observations:

Special memories:

Whiskeytown Falls

Widely recognized as one of the best waterfalls in Northern California, Whiskey Falls is a 220-foot high waterfall. It is reached via a strenuous 1.7 mile uphill hike on the James K. Carr Trail (3.4-mile round trip). The hike itself is beautiful, climbing through dense forests and traversing over a few small bridges before arriving at the falls.

Whiskeytown Falls is one of four waterfalls in the park and is the tallest and most visited. Shade is abundant, but it is very hot during the summer.

Best time to visit: Spring and early summer

Pass/Permit/Fees: $10 weekly pass required

Closest city or town: French Gulch, California

How to get there: From Whiskeytown Visitor Center, turn left onto CA- 299 West for 8.4 miles. Go left onto Crystal Creek Rd. and drive 3.7 miles. The trailhead and parking area will be on the left.

GPS Coordinates: 40.6264° N, 122.6692° W

Did you know? Whiskey Falls was recently discovered by park managers of the Whiskeytown Recreation Area in 2004. Prior to that, the waterfalls were a local secret and had been mis-mapped.

Journal:

Date(s) Visited:

Weather
conditions:

Who you were with:

Nature observations:

Special memories:

Yosemite Falls

Located in the Yosemite National Park, Yosemite Falls is one of the world's tallest waterfalls at 2,425 feet. It is actually three waterfalls: Upper Yosemite Fall, the middle cascades, and Lower Yosemite Falls.

The waterfall is viewable from numerous places around Yosemite Valley. There's a one-mile loop trail that leads to the base of Lower Yosemite Falls. You can also hike to the top if you're up for a strenuous, all-day hike.

Best time to visit: Spring for peak water flow

Pass/Permit/Fees: $35 per car, $30 per motorcycle, and $15 on foot, horseback, bike, or bus. Good for seven days.

Closest city or town: El Portal, California

How to get there: Of the five entrances into Yosemite National Park, there are two that will lead you to Yosemite Valley: 1) Big Oak Flat Entrance– take Hwy. 120 east into the park or 2) The Arch Rock Entrance– take Hwy. 140 east into the park

GPS Coordinates: 37.7566° N, 119.5969° W

Did you know? The waterfall of Yosemite Falls is fed entirely by snowmelt, so it completely dries up by August.

Journal:

Date(s) Visited:

Weather conditions:

Who you were with:

Nature observations:

Special memories:

Central Region

Bear Gulch Cave

Bear Gulch Cave is one of two unique caves in Pinnacles National Park. It and Balconies Cave were created by cave-ins rather than lava flow. Bear Gulch Cave is a talus cave, which consists of open spaces among large rocks and boulders.

There are a few converging trails around Bear Gulch, so watch your signs carefully at trail splits. Overall, it is a short and easy trail with beautiful rock formation and the unique experience of the talus cave.

Best time to visit: Usually open mid-July through mid-May, depending on the presence of bats.

Pass/Permit/Fees: $15 to enter the park

Closest city or town: King City, California

How to get there: The trail is accessed from the east entrance of the park, past Bear Gulch Day Use Area. Begin hiking south from this area, and after 0.2 miles, take the left split. Make sure to have a flashlight or headlamp.

GPS Coordinates: 40.8549° N, 122.7200° W

Did you know? Bear Gulch Cave provides a home to a colony of Townsend's big-eared bats, a sensitive species.

Journal:

Date(s) Visited:

Weather
conditions:

Who you were with:

Nature observations:

Special memories:

Bishop Creek

Located in Inyo National Forest in the eastern Sierra Nevada, Bishop Creek is a 10.1-mile stream that has three forks, which all flow into lakes: North Lake, Sabrina Lake, and South Lake. There is also a reservoir called Intake Two along the way, and Bishop Creek meets Owens River past the city of Bishop.

Because there are several incredible views in this area, it is recommended to camp for a few days for time to explore. Fishing, bouldering, and motorboating are popular activities, along with scenic hiking. There is parking near each of the lakes, and the canyon, surrounding mountains, and alpine forests offer beautiful settings for a camping trip.

Best time to visit: Fall

Pass/Permit/Fees: $5 per person entrance fee

Closest city or town: Bishop, California

How to get there: To Bishop Creek Lodge and Resort: take State Rte. 168 West and turn off at the South Lake. Turn off at the end of the road.

GPS Coordinates: 37.265833° N, 118.578056° W

Did you know? Bishop Creek is at an elevation of about 7,400 feet.

Journal:

Date(s) Visited:

Weather conditions:

Who you were with:

Nature observations:

Special memories:

Crystal Cave

Crystal Cave is a marble karst cave, ornate and polished by streams and decorated with stalactites and stalagmites galore. The main attraction of Sequoia National Park, Crystal Cave, is only open in the summer. The road to the cave, Crystal Cave Road, is narrow and winding, so no large vehicles over 22 feet or with towing trailers allowed. Plan about two hours total for the visit: one hour to tour and 30 minutes each way to drive the road.

The cave is beautifully maintained and is about a one-hour tour. The trail to the start of the cave is a half-mile of gorgeous views. The highly detailed formations in the cave are extremely fragile, so the only way to visit the cave is on a guided tour. The temperature inside the cave is about 50°F, so a jacket is advised.

Best time to visit: Summer

Pass/Permit/Fees: $18 per person; best to book a tour in advance; tickets are not sold at the cave.

Closest city or town:

How to get there: Located near Giant Forest in the park. Take Generals Hwy. Turn onto Crystal Cave Rd. and drive 6.5 miles to the parking area.

GPS Coordinates: 36.5874° N, 118.8304° W

Did you know? Crystal Cave contains over three miles of passages.

Journal:

Date(s) Visited:

Weather
conditions:

Who you were with:

Nature observations:

Special memories:

Devils Postpile

Located near Mammoth Mountain is the geologic wonder, Devils Postpile. This formation is a rare sight of massive rocks that seemingly jut out of the earth's surface. It is one of the world's finest examples of columnar basalt, and the columns tower up to 60 feet and are 2-3.5 feet in diameter.

These unique rock formations are hexagonal at the top, which can be viewed up close as a part of the hike. Devils Postpile Trail is full of beautiful views and has the option to continue to Rainbow Falls, too. The area is protected as a National Monument as of 1911.

Best time to visit: Mid-June to mid-October

Pass/Permit/Fees: $ 8-day pass, $16 three-day pass, and $40 season pass.

Closest city or town: Mammoth Lakes, California

How to get there: Most visitors must park at the Mammoth Mountain Ski Area and use the mandatory shuttle, which operates mid-June through the Wednesday after Labor Day. By car: From U.S. Hwy. 395, drive 10 miles west on State Rte. 203 to Minaret Vista. Go eight miles. There are few exceptions to the shuttle bus.

GPS Coordinates: 37.6251° N, 119.0850° W

Did you know? The hexagonal columns are believed to have formed 10,000 years ago from a cliff of cooled lava.

Journal:

Date(s) Visited:

Weather conditions:

Who you were with:

Nature observations:

Special memories:

Fossil Falls

Being that there aren't any fossils or waterfalls, Fossil Falls is a bit of a misnomer. Thousands of years ago, the Owens River flowed through the Coso Range area and interacted with lava from nearby volcanoes, creating the falls that are now sculpted black lava rocks. Glaciers also played a role in shaping this unique area.

The trail to the falls is only 0.2 miles and full of volcanic rock. The falls are barren, so you won't be looking for water, but rather a strange rock cluster that was once a waterfall. The rock gives way to a 60–70-foot drop through a volcanic rock canyon that climbers love.

The short trail leads you to observe the falls from above, and there is also a trail to descend the falls. Proceed with cautious footing and be wary of loose rocks on the descending trail.

Best time to visit: Fall or spring

Pass/Permit/Fees: Free to visit, $6 overnight at the campground

Closest city or town: Little Lake

How to get there: Drive north on Hwy. 395 past Pearsonville. Watch for signs that note Fossil Falls on the right. Turn and travel to the small, dirt parking lot, where you'll find a map and facilities.

GPS Coordinates: 35.9699° N, 117.9090° W

Did you know? This desert location makes for spectacular night views of the sky.

Journal:

Date(s) Visited:

Weather
conditions:

Who you were with:

Nature observations:

Special memories:

General Grant Grove

Located in Kings Canyon National Park, General Grant Grove is a grove of giant sequoia trees. Its namesake tree, General Grant, is the second-largest known tree in the world at 267 feet tall and 107 feet around. The tree was named in 1867 after Ulysses S. Grant.

Declared a National Shrine by President Eisenhower in 1956, General Grant Tree is the only example of a living shrine in the United States.

There are several trail options to view the giant sequoias in the grove, including the General Grant Tree Trail and panoramic views of the area.

Best time to visit: June-August

Pass/Permit/Fees: $35 vehicle, $40 motorcycle, and $20 individual on foot or bicycle.

Closest city or town: Fresno, California

How to get there: To the General Grant Tree trailhead: From Fresno, drive east on Rte. 180. After 50 miles, you will reach Big Stump Entrance Station for King Canyons National Park. Continue on Rte. 180 until Grant Tree Rd. Turn left and proceed about a mile to the Grant Grove Parking area.

GPS Coordinates: 36.7483° N, 118.9712° W

Did you know? President Calvin Coolidge designated General Grant as the nation's Christmas tree on April 28, 1926.

Journal:

Date(s) Visited:

Weather conditions:

Who you were with:

Nature observations:

Special memories:

General Sherman

General Sherman is located in Sequoia National Park and is the largest tree in the world. While it is not the tallest at 275 feet tall, its diameter is 36 feet at the base, making it the overall largest tree measured by volume. It is estimated to be 2,300 to 2,500 years old and is a giant sequoia tree.

The trail leading to General Sherman is appropriately named the Sherman Tree Trail and features a walk-up platform for a closer view of the behemoth tree. There are also several other trails to explore in the surrounding area for more views of the giant sequoia trees.

Best time to visit: Visit late May or early September to avoid crowds; summertime for the shuttle service.

Pass/Permit/Fees: Entrance to the park: $35 per vehicle, $30 per motorcycle, and $20 per individual on foot or bike. Valid for seven days.

Closest city or town: Three Rivers, California

How to get there: From the Giant Forest Museum, head north on Generals Hwy. Turn right onto Wolverton Rd. and right again toward the Sherman Tree Trail. The road ends at the parking lot.

GPS Coordinates: 36.5819 N°, 118.7511° W

Did you know? General Sherman is still growing, adding about 0.4 inches in diameter each year.

Journal:

Date(s) Visited:

Weather conditions:

Who you were with:

Nature observations:

Special memories:

Kings Canyon

The drive into Kings Canyon is incredibly scenic, traversing massive canyons, passing waterfalls, and following along a river. Down in the heart of Kings Canyon is a walking trail into Zumwalt Meadows, which is surrounded by mountainous views.

The drive to reach Road's End, the end of Hwy. 180 is called the Kings Canyon Scenic Byway. At 50 miles long, the drive starts at Hume Lake District and takes you into the valley of Kings Canyon and Cedar Grove, and it is full of beautiful scenery. You can also visit Grizzly Falls, which is near Cedar Grove.

Kings Canyon Panoramic Point is also a beautiful view to consider visiting. The loop trail near Cedar Grove that takes you to the point features wildflowers and is an easy trek.

Best time to visit: Mid-May through mid-October

Pass/Permit/Fees: $35 per vehicle, $40 per motorcycle, and $20 per individual on foot or bicycle.

Closest city or town: Visalia, California

How to get there: Hwy. 180 enters King Canyon National Park from the west via Fresno.

GPS Coordinates: 36.8879° N, 118.5551° W

Did you know? Kings Canyon is deeper than the Grand Canyon and reaches up to 8,200 feet deep.

Journal:

Date(s) Visited:

Weather
conditions:

Who you were with:

Nature observations:

Special memories:

Mammoth Mountain

Due to its location down in the Sierra Crest, Mammoth Mountain gets an unusually large amount of snowfall and is home to the Mammoth Mountain Ski Area. During the winter months, come ski, snowboard, and snowmobile at the highest ski resort in California.

It is a four-season resort, so the summer offers activities of its own, including guided climbing, mountain biking, and scenic trails. Mammoth Mountain is also home to the premier bike park in the U.S., Mammoth Bike Park.

The gondola rides operate all year and are a perfect opportunity for aerial views and a ride to the summit. A few miles from the mountain lies the Mammoth Lakes Basin, a favorite destination for hiking, biking, and fishing.

Best time to visit: Anytime, depending on activities

Pass/Permit/Fees: Lift tickets $30-$80, Season Passes $399-$999

Closest city or town: Mammoth Lakes, California

How to get there: Take Hwy. 395 north or south to the city of Mammoth Lakes. A free shuttle service will get you around.

GPS Coordinates: 37.6308° N, 119.0326° W

Did you know? At 11,059 feet in elevation, Mammoth Mountain is a lava dome complex, which means it has a circular mound shape formed from a series of volcanic eruptions around 60,000 years ago.

Journal:

Date(s) Visited:

Weather
conditions:

Who you were with:

Nature observations:

Special memories:

McWay Falls

Highway 1 along the Bur Sur Coast is called "the longest and most scenic stretch of undeveloped coastline in the contiguous U.S." Along the way is an overlook trail that features a stunning waterfall.

McWay Falls is an 80-foot waterfall dropping onto a lovely beach cove. Visitors are prohibited on the beach area, so the cove remains natural. The water flows all year round and, during high tide, it can become a tide fall that falls directly into the ocean.

There are two ways to access the McWay Falls Overlook Trail, a 0.6 mile round trip trail to view the falls. You can either park along Hwy. 1 for free, or you can access the trail while visiting the Julia Pfeiffer Burns State Park. The park also contains Canyon Falls too.

Best time to visit: Spring or early summer for the wildflowers

Pass/Permit/Fees: $10 entry fee to Julia Pfeiffer Burns State Park

Closest city or town: Big Sur, California

How to get there: From Ragged Point, drive north on Hwy. 1 for 37 miles to Julia Burns State Park. The park is about eight miles south of Big Sur. The trailhead is just south of the park entrance, on the west side of the road.

GPS Coordinates: 36.1578° N, 121.6722° W

Did you know? McWay Falls is one of two tide falls in California, with the other being Alamere Falls.

Journal:

Date(s) Visited:

Weather conditions:

Who you were with:

Nature observations:

Special memories:

Moaning Cavern

Named for the rock formations and sounds caused by dripping water, Moaning Cavern is a deep, vertical cave chamber. One of the few caves of this nature in the United States, it is one of the longest rappels in the country. This cave is tall enough that it could hold the Statue of Liberty.

At Moaning Caverns Adventure Park, there are guided walking tours, such as the Spiral Tour, which descends 16 stories underground via the spiral staircase. The Expedition Trip takes you through the unlit areas of the cave where you'll climb, crawl, and squeeze your way through. The Adventure Trip features the 165-foot rappel to the bottom and takes about three hours.

Best time to visit: Winter

Pass/Permit/Fees: Spiral Tour $20, Expedition Trip $95, and Adventure Trip $200-$300.

Closest city or town: Vallecito, California

How to get there: From Angels Camp, take Hwy. 4 East ten minutes, then turn right onto Parrotts Ferry Rd. at the Moaning Cavern sign. Drive one mile, then turn right onto Moaning Cave Rd.

GPS Coordinates: 38.0690° N, 120.4661° W

Did you know? Moaning Cavern holds archaeological significance, as some of the oldest human remains known in the U.S. were discovered here.

Journal:

Date(s) Visited:

Weather conditions:

Who you were with:

Nature observations:

Special memories:

Mobius Arch

Mobius Arch is found in Alabama Hills Recreation Area, a site where many cowboy movies have been filmed. The arch is a circular rock formation that is large and unique and surrounded by beautiful geological formations. The window of the arch is about 6.5 feet high and perfectly frames Mt. Whitney when viewed from the correct angle.

The Mobius Arch Loop Trail is easy to travel and only 0.6 miles, and the drive from Lone Pine is short and sweet. This makes Mobius Arch ideal for a pit stop on your way to other sites in the area, such as Mt. Whitney. The trail is well-marked with brown posts and stones. After Mobius Arch, there is a trail to Lathe Arch if you're feeling extra adventurous.

Best time to visit: May-October

Pass/Permit/Fees: Free

Closest city or town: Lone Pine, California

How to get there: From Lone Pine, go west on Whitey Portal Rd. and turn right onto Movie Flat Rd. Once on Movie Flat Rd., stay on the widest dirt road, avoiding side roads. At the big split, stay to the right to the parking area.

GPS Coordinates: 36.6113° N, 118.1249° W

Did you know? Mobius Arch got its name from the way it folds over, like a Mobius strip.

Journal:

Date(s) Visited:

Weather
conditions:

Who you were with:

Nature observations:

Special memories:

Morro Rock

Located in Morro Bay, this State Historic Landmark has formed around 23 million years ago from an extinct volcano. Morro Rock is a volcanic plug at the entrance to Morro Bay Harbor.

The beach the rock is located on is named Morro Rock Beach, and the rock is perched on the edge of the Pacific Ocean. There are over six miles of unspoiled beaches to enjoy. You can drive to the base of Morro Rock, but note that climbing Morro Rock is prohibited by law.

There are various recreational activities to do while you're in Morro Bay, including oceanside golf, sailing, kayaking, hiking, fishing, whale watching, biking, surfing, and birdwatching. The Cloisters Wetland loop trail offers scenic views on your way to the rock.

Best time to visit: Anytime

Pass/Permit/Fees: Free to visit, camping available

Closest city or town: Morro Bay, California

How to get there: To the trailhead: from Hwy. 1 in Morro Bay, exit on San Jacinto St., and drive west to Coral Ave. Turn left and drive ⅓ mile to Cloisters Park, a parking area on the left.

GPS Coordinates: 35.3694° N, 120.8677° W

Did you know? The rock is about 576 feet tall and is the most visible in the chain of nine extinct volcanoes called the Nine Sisters.
Journal:

Date(s) Visited:

Weather
conditions:

Who you were with:

Nature observations:

Special memories:

Mount Whitney

Mountains are wonders of nature in any adventure guide, but you can't miss the tallest peak in the lower 48 states. At its peak awaits a grand view of the Sierra Nevada Mountains.

Because Mt. Whitney is on the far eastern boundary of Sequoia National Park, there is a chain of mountains through the center that block views of Whitney from park roads. A good view can be seen at the Interagency Visitor Center on Hwy. 395.

Adventurers can also summit the mountain from the west in Sequoia National Park or from the east in Inyo National Forest. Most people climb from the east side, Inyo, with the shortest and most popular route being from Whitney Portal, 13 miles west of Lone Pine, California.

Best time to visit: July-October

Pass/Permit/Fees: Permits are required for hiking and backpacking from May 1-November 1 and are distributed via lottery. $6 per application, $15 per person.

Closest city or town: Lone Pine, California

How to get there: Take U.S. 395 to Lone Pine, then turn west onto Whitney Portal Rd. Drive for 13 miles to the trailhead.

GPS Coordinates: 36.5785° N, 118.2923° W

Did you know? The view at the summit offers stunning views of Death Valley National Park.

Journal:

Date(s) Visited:

Weather conditions:

Who you were with:

Nature observations:

Special memories:

71

Natural Bridges State Beach

This 65-acre state park, named for the natural bridges formed across sections of the beach, also features tidal pools and monarch migrations. The three original arches formed over a million years ago and were once part of a large cliff that jutted out into the sea. Wave and wind erosion cut away two into islands, and only the one from the middle of the bridge remains.

The Monarch Grove in the park has been declared a Natural Preserve and is home to up to 150,000 monarch butterflies from October through early February.

Best time to visit: Late October through November for monarchs, open year-round

Pass/Permit/Fees: $10 vehicle day-use fee, $10 parking

Closest city or town: Santa Cruz, California

How to get there: Take Swift Street west from Hwy. 1 or follow West Cliff Dr. north along the bluffs until you reach Natural Bridges.

GPS Coordinates: 36.9503° N, 122.0576° W

Did you know? The tidepools are full of colorful sea anemones, sea stars, and hermit crabs.

Journal:

Date(s) Visited:

Weather
conditions:

Who you were with:

Nature observations:

Special memories:

Pfeiffer Beach

You'll want to visit this hidden gem while near the Big Sur Coastline. Go at sunset for the best photo up with The Keyhole Arch. The Keyhole Arch is magnificent, with waves crashing through the natural arch. There are other dramatic rock formations besides Keyhole Arch at Pfeiffer Beach.

At the north end of the beach, there is unique purple sand from the manganese garnet rocks in the cliffs. Swimming is not advised due to potentially dangerous currents, and the water is cold.

A bit off the beaten path, Pfeiffer Beach is well worth the drive. It's a spot that's easy to miss, being that it isn't sign-posted or visible from the highway. No camping or fires permitted.

Best time to visit: For the picturesque sunset, visit mid-December through mid-January.

Pass/Permit/Fees: $12 day-use fee, $12 parking

Closest city or town: Big Sur, California

How to get there: Take Hwy. 1 to Sycamore Canyon Rd., which is in between Big Sur Ranger Station and the Post Office.

GPS Coordinates: 36.2381° N, 121.8162° W

Did you know? The extreme north side of the beach is on federal land and is sometimes clothing optional.

Journal:

Date(s) Visited:

Weather conditions:

Who you were with:

Nature observations:

Special memories:

Point Lobos

Often referred to as "the crown jewel of the State Park Systems," Point Lobos State Natural Reserve attracts over a million people each year. A natural preserve great for sightseeing, photography, nature study, scuba diving, jogging, and painting. It is also scientifically interesting. Rare plant communities, unique geological formations, endangered archaeological sites, and land and sea flora and fauna are all found in the area. As one of the richest marine habitats in California, the Point Lobos State Marine Preserve can only be explored by certified divers, and reservations are requested.

If you have an hour to spend, take the Cypress Grove Trail for excellent rocky shoreline views, sea lions and sea otters, and ancient Monterey Cypress trees. There are several trails to explore if you'd like to spend the day.

Best time to visit: Fall or spring

Pass/Permit/Fees: $10 day-use fee, diving fees depend

Closest city or town: Carmel-by-the-Sea, California

How to get there: The entrance is just south of Carmel-by-the-Sea on Hwy. 1.

GPS Coordinates: 36.5159° N, 121.9382° W

Did you know? The name is derived from the offshore rocks at Punta de Los Lobos Marinos, or Point of the SeaWolves, for the sea lions around.

Journal:

Date(s) Visited:

Weather
conditions:

Who you were with:

Nature observations:

Special memories:

Southern Region

Amboy Crater

Amboy Crater is an extinct cinder cone volcano that overlooks a lava field. It is estimated to be around 79,000 years old and is found in the eastern Mojave Desert. In 1973, the crater was designated the Amboy Crater National Natural Landmark.

For a vast view of the surrounding landscapes, you can hike to the top of the crater. It is 944 feet above sea level, 250 feet above the surrounding land, and accessible using the Western Cone Trail.

Best time to visit: Winter or early spring

Pass/Permit/Fees: No admission fee

Closest city or town: Ambroy, California

How to get there: Off the historic Rte. 66. From Barstow, take I-40 West to Exit 50. Right on Crucero Rd. and immediately left onto Rte. 66. Go 26 miles to the crater.

GPS Coordinates: 34.5439° N, 115.7911° W

Did you know? The volcano last erupted 10,000 years ago, transforming the surrounding landscape.

Journal:

Date(s) Visited:

Weather
conditions:

Who you were with:

Nature observations:

Special memories:

Artist's Palette - Death Valley

A unique venture in Death Valley National Park is Artist's Drive. This drive takes you through canyons and past mountains that are covered in various colors. The main stop at the end is Artist's Palette, which features the most colorful rocks and soil.

The oxidation of metals and elements from the ground of the area produces vibrant colors. The entire route is quite scenic and is a nine-mile, one-way loop. There is a parking lot along the way so you can access the viewpoint on foot.

Best time to visit: November-April

Pass/Permit/Fees: To enter Death Valley National Park: $30 per vehicle, $25 per motorcycle, $15 on foot, bike, or horse.

Closest city or town: Pahrump, California

How to get there: Artist's Drive is off of Badwater Road, north of Devils' Golf Course, and south of Furnace Creek.

GPS Coordinates: 42.5306° N, 75.5235° W

Did you know? The colorful oxidation of the minerals is evidence of the area's explosive, volcanic periods.

Journal:

Date(s) Visited:

Weather
conditions:

Who you were with:

Nature observations:

Special memories:

Badwater - Death Valley

Death Valley National Park is full of mountains, salt formations, sand dunes, and an enormous crater. As one of the top national parks, it can be featured in its own guide. There are several driving routes that lead through some of the main sites throughout the park. The most popular drive is the Badwater Road.

Badwater Basin — the lowest point of land in the western hemisphere — is 282 feet below sea level and hot all year round. Surrounded by mountains, Badwater Lake is shallow and rimmed with salt.

The conditions and time of year affect the water level, and when there's no water, you can walk out into the basin's thick layer of salt on the valley floor. There's also a boardwalk across the basin.

Best time to visit: Winter or late fall

Pass/Permit/Fees: $25 per vehicle, good for seven days

Closest city or town: Beatty, California; Los Angeles is the closest major city to the park.

How to get there: From Furnace Creek, drive 17 miles south on Badwater Rd. The parking area will be on the right.

GPS Coordinates: 36.2461° N, 116.8185° W

Did you know? Badwater basin is home to a species of minute salt marsh snail endemic called the Badwater Snail.

Journal:

Date(s) Visited:

Weather
conditions:

Who you were with:

Nature observations:

Special memories:

Big Bear Lake

The Big Bear Lake area is more than a lake; it is also the name of the nearby alpine town in an area with forestry and mountains too. The San Bernardino Forest and Mountains surround the city, offering various recreational activities.

The four-season mountain lake offers fishing year-round and 22 miles of shoreline. You can paddleboard, kayak, and water ski, too. Along with the seven-mile lake, Big Bear Mountain Resort has skiing and snowboarding in the winter and mountain biking in the summer. There are 60+ miles of cross-country trails for hikers and bikers and recreational paths for every level. The area also features zip-wire tours, helicopter tours, and the Big Bear Jeep Experience.

Best time to visit: Spring for the lake, winter for snow sports

Pass/Permit/Fees: Lake use permit required for vessels (fees vary); fishing permit required. Adventure Pass is $5.

Closest city or town: San Bernardino, California

How to get there: From I-80 or CA-210, you can choose between CA-330, which becomes the CA-18 and is faster, or take CA-38 through Mentone for less traffic.

GPS Coordinates: 34.2439° N, 116.9114° W

Did you know? The lake was actually made using dams.

Journal:

Date(s) Visited:

Weather conditions:

Who you were with:

Nature observations:

Special memories:

Cima Dome

Famous for its impressively even dome shape, Cima Dome is a massive 70-acre dome that covers 70 square miles. Its lack of foliage creates a smoothness that looks like the fisheye lens of a camera for as far as you can see. Its nearly perfect symmetry rises 1,500 feet above the surrounding Mojave Desert.

Teutonia Peak Trail winds through the densest Joshua Tree Forest in the world and to the top of a rocky 5,755-foot mountain on the edge of Cima Dome. There are also silver mines covered by grates along the way.

You can also view this unusual geological feature from a distance looking northwest from Cedar Canyon Road, 2.5 miles east of Kelso Cima Road.

Best time to visit: March-April for carpets of wildflowers

Pass/Permit/Fees: Free

Closest city or town: Cima, California

How to get there: From Cima, drive north on Cima Rd. for six miles to the trailhead. From the 15 Freeway, exit Cima Rd. and drive south for 11 miles to the turnout. The trail is on the south side of the road.

GPS Coordinates: 35.2894° N, 115.5853° W

Did you know? Cima Volcanic Field is west of Cima Dome and consists of around 40 volcanic cones and near 60 lava flows.

Journal:

Date(s) Visited:

Weather conditions:

Who you were with:

Nature observations:

Special memories:

Imperial Sand Dunes

Formed by windblown sands of the ancient Lake Cahuilla, the Imperial Sand Dunes are the largest mass of sand dunes in California. Dunes here reach heights of 300 feet, and the dune system extends for more than 40 miles in a band.

The Imperial Sand Dunes Recreational Area (ISDRA) offers off-road action for off-highway vehicles, fabulous scenery, solitude, and rare wildlife. There's also the North Algodones Dunes Wilderness which encompasses 26,000 acres and offers a tranquil alternative to the busy central area. This remote area is open to walking and horseback riding in the dunes.

Best time to visit: Winter for moderate temperatures

Pass/Permit/Fees: Permits required October 1-April 15. $35 per week in advance, $50 onsite.

Closest city or town: El Centro, California

How to get there: Access to the Imperial Sand Dunes Recreation Area is best made along Hwy. 78 located East of Brawley, California or along Interstate 8 west of Yuma, Arizona

GPS Coordinates: 32.9734° N, 115.1727° W

Did you know? The sand dunes have been featured in several movies, including *Star Wars: Return of the Jedi* and *Jumanji 3.*

Journal:

Date(s) Visited:

Weather
conditions:

Who you were with:

Nature observations:

Special memories:

Inspiration Point - Channel Islands

At 14 miles off the coast of California at its shortest distance, Channel Islands National Park is a series of five islands that are remote and feature untouched beauty. Inspiration Point is found on Anacapa Island.

The Landing Cove is the area where the boat backs in to pick up and drop off on Anapacapa. There is a kelp forest, and you can kayak to explore the caves and island from the water, and at the southern tip of the island is a beautiful lighthouse. The main highlight of the island is Inspiration Point, which offers the stunning viewpoint looking over the middle island and vistas of the two other parts of the Anacapa. There are also plenty of coves and the arch rock on the south side of the island to explore, along with the diverse wildlife, including dolphins, whales, and seals.

Best time to visit: Any time of year

Pass/Permit/Fees: $60-$85 per day for a round-trip boat ride, $80 for a camping trip and round-trip boat ride, and $15 for camping.

Closest city or town: Ventura, California

How to get there: Island Packers is the public boat transportation service. To get there, take Hwy. 101 to Harbor Blvd. and proceed to Spinnaker Drive. Turn right and follow the "Island Tours/Island Packers" sign.

GPS Coordinates: 34.0044° N, 119.3996° W

Did you know? There are island foxes on the Channel Islands.

Journal:

Date(s) Visited:

Weather conditions:

Who you were with:

Nature observations:

Special memories:

Joshua Tree National Park

Appropriately named the Joshua Tree National Park, this park features trees and giant granite boulders, and mountains. The landscape has often been described as lunar, and people often use terms like spiritual or magical to describe how they feel about this area.

The most popular things to do are hiking among the trees, rock climbing, stargazing, and photography. The park is located where the Mojave and Colorado Deserts meet. The Hidden Valley area and trail are easily accessible and scenic with the trees and the monolith known as the Great Burrito. The entire park is nearly 800,000 acres, so there is plenty to see. Skull Rock and Keys Views are two favorite destinations.

Best time to visit: Visit in the spring or fall or avoid the searing heat of Southern California.

Pass/Permit/Fees: October-May

Closest city or town: Twentynine Palms, California

How to get there: Approach the park from Interstate 10 or CA-62. There are three park entrances, with the north entrance being in Twentynine Palms.

GPS Coordinates: 33.8734° N, 115.9010° W

Did you know? The park is designated an International Dark Sky Park and offers a great chance to view the stars and Milky Way.

Journal:

Date(s) Visited:

Weather
conditions:

Who you were with:

Nature observations:

Special memories:

Lava Tube - Mojave Desert

Lava tubes are a natural phenomenon that all adventurers should experience. This lava tube in the Mojave Desert is the subject of many photographs. It is famous for the small holes in the ceiling that allow a cascade of light into the dark cave. The small dust particles in the air catch the light as an awe-inspiring beam for visitors to enjoy the subterranean cave.

The five-mile dirt road is a bit rough, so you'll want a high-profile vehicle. The cave is about 500 feet long, 3 feet tall at its shortest, and about 10 feet wide in other places. The hike to the entrance is only about a quarter of a mile and takes you over tar-black volcanic rocks on a small incline. There is a metal ladder of about 16 steps that descend into the tube. Bring a flashlight.

Best time to visit: Midday, in the spring when the sun is overhead

Pass/Permit/Fees: Free

Closest city or town: Baker, California

How to get there: Trailhead is accessed from Aiken Mine Rd., which can be reached from the north on Hwy. 15 via Baker, California, or from the south on Hwy. 40 via Kelbaker Rd. Roads may be impassable in wet conditions.

GPS Coordinates: 35.2163° N, 115.7515° W

Did you know? This lava tube formed approximately 7.6 million years ago.

Journal:

Date(s) Visited:

Weather
conditions:

Who you were with:

Nature observations:

Special memories:

Mount San Jacinto

Standing at 10,084 feet above sea level, Mount San Jacinto is the second highest peak in Southern California. The entire area is scenic. Being located in a high-country wilderness area, hikers enjoy the contrast it offers with the San Bernardino National Forest surrounding the mountain range and looking down into the desert. The Cactus-to-Clouds Trail takes you from the desert to the subalpine peak.

The San Jacinto Peak Trail is an 11 mile round trip with a 2,300-foot elevation gain that takes around five to six hours to complete. This trailhead is accessed via the Palm Springs Aerial Tramway and is one of the lower effort trails, although still difficult. A second, more intense trail is the San Jacinto Peak Loop Trail, which is 18.5 miles and only recommended for very experienced adventurers.

Best time to visit: May-October

Pass/Permit/Fees: Day Use Wilderness Permit required and free. Wilderness Camping Permits are $5.

Closest city or town: Palm Springs, California

How to get there: To Mt. San Jacinto State Park: Take Hwy. CA-111 North to I-10 west to Hwy. 243 South to the park.

GPS Coordinates: 33.8145° N, 116.6792° W

Did you know? Mount San Jacinto is one of 59 named mountains in the range.

Journal:

Date(s) Visited:

Weather
conditions:

Who you were with:

Nature observations:

Special memories:

Painted Canyon

The Ladder Canyon Trail is a 4.5-mile loop that passes through a slot canyon, goes up a ridge, and leads you along the bottom of Big Painted Canyon. This is a two to three-hour trek, so be sure to take some water.

With the trail surface of sand and loose gravel coupled with climbing ladders to access part of the trail, getting to Painted Canyon will take some effort, but it is totally worth it. The views from the top are amazing, and the canyons are beautiful. The trails feature a waterfall and are rated as moderate.

Best time to visit: October-April

Pass/Permit/Fees: Free

Closest city or town: 40 miles southeast of Palm Springs. Outside of the desert city of Mecca.

How to get there: From Palm Springs, take Hwy. 111 East to Mecca, towards the Salton Sea. Turn left at 66th Ave. and continue through Mecca. 66th becomes Box Canyon Rd. From there, watch for a sign for Painted Canyon Rd., where you will turn left. The dirt road will take you to the parking area.

GPS Coordinates: 33° 35' 23.9532'' N, 116° 0' 59.6736'' W

Did you know? The colorful walls of the exposed rock layers of the canyon include pink, red, grey, brown, and green colors.

Journal:

Date(s) Visited:

Weather conditions:

Who you were with:

Nature observations:

Special memories:

Racetrack- Death Valley

One of the most famous Death Valley attractions, Racetrack, is named for the tracks left behind by stones that seemingly move all on their own. Nicknamed the "sailing stones," the synchronized, linear tracks had largely been a mystery until 2016.

The dry, desolate lake bed, or playa, is one of the more undisturbed areas due to its remote location. This geological phenomenon is only accessible via an all-day trek in a four-wheel-drive vehicle.

After arriving at the north end of the Racetrack and Grandstand parking area, the short walk to the Grandstand can be rewarding. To see the rocks, drive two miles south of the Grandstand parking area. Walkabout a half of a mile toward the southeast of the playa for the best views of the rocks and their tracks.

Best time to visit: September-June

Pass/Permit/Fees: $25 per vehicle for seven days

Closest city or town: Pahrump, Nevada & Furnace Creek, California

How to get there: From Furnace Valley Visitor Center, drive north. Near the parking lot of Ubehebe Crater is the turn-off for Racetrack Valley Rd. It is 27 miles to the playa and the Grandstand parking area.

GPS Coordinates: 36.6813° N, 117.5627° W

Did you know? Some of the rocks in the playa weigh as much as 700 pounds.

Journal:

Date(s) Visited:

Weather
conditions:

Who you were with:

Nature observations:

Special memories:

Crystal Cove State Park

One of the most gorgeous coastlines in California, Laguna Beach is full of cliff formations, caves, rock arches, and tide pools. There are several amazing places to visit along Laguna Beach, with one of them being Crystal Cove.

This state park features 3.2 miles of shoreline and 2,400 acres of backcountry wilderness. Mountain biking, horseback riding, and hiking are great activities for the inland, and divers enjoy the underwater experience at the beach. Tidepools and sandy coves, rocky reefs, ridges, and canyons can all be found in the area.

This is also a great park for camping. The scenic Moro Campground is a great established place to camp, and there are also 58 total sites for RVs, van conversions, and tents.

Best time to visit: Summertime is pretty crowded, consider the off-season.

Pass/Permit/Fees: Day-use parking is $15

Closest city or town: Laguna Beach, California

How to get there: Located right off the Pacific Coast Hwy. between Corona del Mar and Laguna Beach.

GPS Coordinates: 33.5766° N, 117.8418° W

Did you know? Crystal Cove is one of the largest remaining open spaces in Orange County, California.

Journal:

Date(s) Visited:

Weather conditions:

Who you were with:

Nature observations:

Special memories:

The Slot Canyon

Located in Anza Borrego State Park, this natural formation is a part of a 2.3-mile loop trail. The Slot is located about two miles down a dirt road that is easy to miss. It is suggested to check in with the visitor's center before heading to the canyon.

Once you find the canyon, you might wish to mark your entrance with rocks to guide you back to your exit. The entrance to the canyon is a slot, and as you proceed, the canyon grows taller and narrower. Along the way is a natural rock bridge across the top of the canyon, and after the bridge, the canyon opens up to a dirt road. You can either walk back around the top or go back through the canyon.

Best time to visit: September-May

Pass/Permit/Fees: $10 entry fee

Closest city or town: Borrego Springs, California

How to get there: From Borrego Springs, drive 11.5 miles southeast on Borrego Springs Rd. Turn left on Rte. 78 East, drive 1.5 miles and turn left on a dirt road marked Buttes Pass. Drive one mile to a fork, and continue to the left up Borrego Mountain Wash. Go another mile to the parking area.

GPS Coordinates: 33.1820° N, 116.2141° W

Did you know? The canyon was formed by flash floods, and at points, the walls reach 40 feet high. The canyon floor gets as narrow as 1 foot.

Journal:

Date(s) Visited:

Weather conditions:

Who you were with:

Nature observations:

Special memories:

Sunset Cliffs

Sunset Cliffs Natural Park spans 68 acres and is in the Point Loma neighborhood of San Diego. This patch of the coast is beautiful and serene, featuring sheer cliffs, beaches, and caves. Be sure to watch your footing when exploring.

A popular surfing spot, this area offers panoramic views of dramatic cliffs along the Pacific Ocean. There are several areas that make for great views, including Ladera Street, Luscomb Point, and Osprey, and even some secret beaches for the explorers.

The Sunset Cliffs Park Trail is 1.7 miles out and back, is good for all skill levels, and is accessible all year. While in the area, there is also an open ceiling sea cave to venture into, but it will only be accessible during the low or negative tide. Even then, plan on getting wet, potentially up to the waist when down below the cliffs.

Best time to visit: Near sunset, April-October

Pass/Permit/Fees: Free

Closest city or town: San Diego, California

How to get there: The best way to access the trail is from 4501 Ladera St. in San Diego.

GPS Coordinates: 32.7252° N, 117.2531° W

Did you know? Sunset Cliffs are near Ocean Beach Pier, the longest pleasure pier on the West Coast.

Journal:

Date(s) Visited:

Weather
conditions:

Who you were with:

Nature observations:

Special memories:

Trona Pinnacles

Located in the California Desert National Conservation Area, this area features tufa towers, tombstones, ridges, and cones that were formed between 10,000 and 100,000 years ago. They were all formed underwater during three different ice ages. These unusual geological features are composed primarily of calcium carbonate or tufa. The tufas are located in the Searles Lake basin, which was once an ancient lakebed. Within the 3,800 acres are 500 tufa spires as high as 140 feet.

Best time to visit: The best time to visit is in the colder months around sunset.

Pass/Permit/Fees: Please refer to the Bureau of Land Management's website for current camping, permit, and fee requirements as they change depending on the season.

Closest city or town: Trona, California

How to get there: Approximately 20 miles east of Ridgecrest, access to the site is from a BLM dirt road, RM 143. On State Rte. 178, go 7.7 miles east past the intersection with Trona-Red Mountain Rd. It is a five-mile-long dirt road usually accessible to most vehicles unless recent heavy rain has fallen.

GPS Coordinates: 35.6177° N, 117.3681° W

Did you know? The Trona Pinnacles have been the backdrop for more than a dozen hit movies, television series, commercials, and music videos.

Journal:

Date(s) Visited:

Weather
conditions:

Who you were with:

Nature observations:

Special memories:

Vasquez Rocks

Located in the desert near Agua Dulce Springs, Vasquez Rocks is an area of 932 acres full of spectacular rock formations. Earthquakes from the San Andreas Fault have twisted and folded rocks into jagged, sharp shapes and strange angles. This landscape is legendary and has been the backdrop for multiple Hollywood movies.

The Vasquez Rocks Natural Area features several trails, with the main attraction being the Famous Rocks, which are found at the heart of the park. There are several routes possible to get to the Famous Rocks, with various extensions to traverse if you want to explore the area. The Pacific Crest Trail is the place to start.

Best time to visit: The shadows of Vasquez Rocks are beautifully dramatic and best witnessed either during the morning in Summer or the afternoon in winter.

Pass/Permit/Fees: Free

Closest city or town: Agua Dolce, California

How to get there: Take CA-14 East, to Exit 15 for Agua Dulce Canyon Rd. Turn left and drive north for 16 miles to a sharp right in the road. Take a right and continue. The road becomes Escondido Canyon Rd. after 0.2 miles. The park is on the right.

GPS Coordinates: 34.4885° N, 118.3207° W

Did you know? The park is named after a famous bandit, Tiburcio Vasquez, who evaded law enforcement by hiding in this area.

Journal:

Date(s) Visited:

Weather
conditions:

Who you were with:

Nature observations:

Special memories:

Other Places

Place: _____

Date(s) Visited:

Weather conditions:

Who you were with:

Nature Observations:

Special Memories:

Place: _____

Date(s) Visited:

Weather conditions:

Who you were with:

Nature Observations:

Special Memories:

Place: _____

Date(s) Visited:

Weather conditions:

Who you were with:

Nature Observations:

Special Memories:

Place: _____

Date(s) Visited:

Weather conditions:

Who you were with:

Nature Observations:

Special Memories:

Place: _____

Date(s) Visited:

Weather conditions:

Who you were with:

Nature Observations:

Special Memories:

Place: _____

Date(s) Visited:

Weather conditions:

Who you were with:

Nature Observations:

Special Memories:

Place: _____

Date(s) Visited:

Weather conditions:

Who you were with:

Nature Observations:

Special Memories:

Place: _____

Date(s) Visited:

Weather conditions:

Who you were with:

Nature Observations:

Special Memories:

Place: _____

Date(s) Visited:

Weather conditions:

Who you were with:

Nature Observations:

Special Memories:

120

Place: _____

Date(s) Visited:

Weather conditions:

Who you were with:

Nature Observations:

Special Memories:

Credit the Incredible Photographers:

Mount Shasta https://search.creativecommons.org/photos/b493061d-7ed5-419e-ba4f-946f03854a47 "3am at Mount Shasta (Long Exposure)" by tim-johnson is licensed with CC BY 2.0. To view a copy of this license, visit https://creativecommons.org/licenses/by/2.0/

The Painted Dunes https://search.creativecommons.org/photos/e38c1442-5bf5-4b2d-bc58-a01dd07454de "Painted Dunes" by cdamundsen is licensed with CC BY-SA 2.0. To view a copy of this license, visit https://creativecommons.org/licenses/by-sa/2.0/

Petrified Forest https://search.creativecommons.org/photos/f5236024-e9cd-4041-90da-1b6e32839920 "Petrified Forest National Wilderness Area South Unit" by PetrifiedForestNPS is marked under CC PDM 1.0. To view the terms, visit https://creativecommons.org/publicdomain/mark/1.0/

Redwood Forest National Park https://search.creativecommons.org/photos/4de3a24c-7233-43a5-b882-d7279d71a5c9 "Redwood Forest" by Photos_by_Angela is licensed with CC BY-SA 2.0. To view a copy of this license, visit https://creativecommons.org/licenses/by-sa/2.0/

Subway Cave https://search.creativecommons.org/photos/66cac744-7e46-497e-bc18-6b5fb3840c6e "subway cave" by beggyberry is licensed with CC BY-ND 2.0. To view a copy of this license, visit https://creativecommons.org/licenses/by-nd/2.0/

Whiskeytown Falls https://search.creativecommons.org/photos/d270491a-1ff7-43bf-b346-b65bed523118 "Whiskey Town Falls" by rajeshn513 is licensed with CC BY 2.0. To view a copy of this license, visit https://creativecommons.org/licenses/by/2.0/

Yosemite Falls https://search.creativecommons.org/photos/f0c7bcd2-6221-45da-b3cb-70a82257b9a5 "Yosemite Falls" by EricHaake is licensed with CC BY 2.0. To view a copy of this license, visit https://creativecommons.org/licenses/by/2.0/

Central Region Bear Gulch Cave https://search.creativecommons.org/photos/35b046d8-1a95-4ec3-af8c-c7edc0b818bb "Bear Gulch" by basheertome is licensed with CC BY 2.0. To view a copy of this license, visit https://creativecommons.org/licenses/by/2.0/

Big Sur Coastline https://search.creativecommons.org/photos/fcc3ad70-b11a-4e02-91f4-8222231195d0 "Big Sur coastline" by | El Caganer - Over 8.5 Million views! is licensed with CC BY 2.0. To view a copy of this license, visit https://creativecommons.org/licenses/by/2.0/

Bishop Creek https://search.creativecommons.org/photos/6a1b9744-15ce-4b6a-8f06-bce76360a6f2 "Golden Bishop Creek, Sierra Nevada, CA 10-18" by inkknife_2000 (11.5 million views) is licensed with CC BY-SA 2.0. To view a copy of this license, visit https://creativecommons.org/licenses/by-sa/2.0/

Crystal Cave https://search.creativecommons.org/photos/a53ef1b5-45e6-40eb-ba76-1103b480464f "Crystal cave" by sergio_leenen is licensed with CC BY-ND 2.0. To view a copy of this license, visit https://creativecommons.org/licenses/by-nd/2.0/

Mount Whitney https://search.creativecommons.org/photos/ebffc4ca-46a8-481d-8102-aa7913cf2fcb "Mount Whitney Summit, 14,505 Feet, California" by Ken Lund is licensed with CC BY-SA 2.0. To view a copy of this license, visit https://creativecommons.org/licenses/by-sa/2.0/

Natural Bridges State Beach https://search.creativecommons.org/photos/52da41a1-3034-4c74-8942-5d8a29df7a25 "2012-01-28 01-29 Santa Cruz 063 Natural Bridges State Beach" by Allie_Caulfield is licensed with CC BY 2.0. To view a copy of this license, visit https://creativecommons.org/licenses/by/2.0/

Pfeiffer Beach https://search.creativecommons.org/photos/fd435837-9b26-4a0f-aa60-af6583828a31 "Pfeiffer Beach Big Sur" by Greg Balzer is licensed with CC BY 2.0. To view a copy of this license, visit https://creativecommons.org/licenses/by/2.0/

Point Lobos https://search.creativecommons.org/photos/f4b4887f-8fd0-470a-90af-4e324fbed2bc "Point Lobos - Cypress Cove" by Jim Bahn is licensed with CC BY 2.0. To view a copy of this license, visit https://creativecommons.org/licenses/by/2.0/

Southern Region Amboy Crater https://search.creativecommons.org/photos/9149f1ea-5263-4c36-aa9d-905bb8039047 "Amboy Crater Area of Critical Environmental Concern, California" by mypubliclands is licensed with CC BY 2.0. To view a copy of this license, visit https://creativecommons.org/licenses/by/2.0/

Artist's Palette - Death Valley https://search.creativecommons.org/photos/ede1bbd7-47d6-4b2d-adc9-9f08f75a1d6c "Artist's Palette" by Paxson Woelber is licensed with CC BY 2.0. To view a copy of this license, visit https://creativecommons.org/licenses/by/2.0/

Badwater - Death Valley https://search.creativecommons.org/photos/cb1b50a9-d6c9-43d0-93e7-2c7eeff95a5a "IMG_2336 - Bad Water - Death Valley" by LaurentGO is licensed with CC BY-SA 2.0. To view a copy of this license, visit https://creativecommons.org/licenses/by-sa/2.0/

Bernardino National Forest https://search.creativecommons.org/photos/4f6f9cc5-2f84-46cd-804b-33e4cfecae35 "Orange and Green - San Bernardino National Forest, CA, USA" by Slipshod Photog is licensed with CC BY-ND 2.0. To view a copy of this license, visit https://creativecommons.org/licenses/by-nd/2.0/

Big Bear Lake https://search.creativecommons.org/photos/d50bffc5-36a8-4478-a2b9-074aaa94cee7 "East Shore, Big Bear Lake, CA 12-14" by inkknife_2000 (11.5 million views) is licensed with CC BY-SA 2.0. To view a copy of this license, visit https://creativecommons.org/licenses/by-sa/2.0/

Cima Dome https://search.creativecommons.org/photos/c7c4865a-12c6-46ca-a65a-e4c7a6889014 "Cima Dome" by cm195902 is licensed with CC BY 2.0. To view a copy of this license, visit https://creativecommons.org/licenses/by/2.0/

Imperial Sand Dunes https://search.creativecommons.org/photos/16fd86f4-f60d-44b9-b895-93871970e221 "#mypubliclandsroadtrip 2016: Something Different, Imperial Sand Dunes" by

Made in the USA
Las Vegas, NV
31 January 2022

42753010R00070